Finance and Economics Discussion Series
Divisions of Research & Statistics and Monetary Affairs
Federal Reserve Board, Washington, D.C.

Gauging the Ability of the FOMC to Respond to Future Recessions

David Reifschneider

2016-068

Please cite this paper as:
Reifschneider, David (2016). "Gauging the Ability of the FOMC to Respond to Future
Recessions," Finance and Economics Discussion Series 2016-068. Washington: Board of
Governors of the Federal Reserve System

Introduction

Current forecasts show the federal funds rate rising gradually over the next few years to a longer-run level of about 3 percent, well below its average over the past 50 years.[1] If these forecasts are accurate, then after the economy returns to normal in a few years the Federal Open Market Committee (FOMC) will apparently be able to cut its policy rate by only 3 percentage points on average in response to adverse shocks, given that the effective lower bound (ELB) on nominal interest rates is approximately zero.[2] By historical standards, this amount of running room would seem rather modest, compared to an average reduction in the federal funds rate of about 5½ percentage points during the past nine recessions. For this reason, some observers have expressed concern that the Federal Reserve will not have adequate scope to respond to future economic downturns, thereby potentially making them deeper and more persistent.

As this note will argue, however, such historical comparisons are misleading for several reasons, including their failure to take account of the demonstrated ability of the FOMC to provide accommodation through large-scale asset purchases and guidance about the future path of the federal funds rate. Given these problems with historical comparisons, this note instead focuses on a different method for gauging the ability of the Federal Reserve to respond to future recessions—model simulations. Specifically, we use FRB/US, a model of the U.S. economy, to

---

[1] In the *Blue Chip Financial Indicators* survey of private financial firms published in June 2016, the consensus forecast showed the federal funds rate converging to 3.2 percent after [2019], while the median of FOMC participants' longer-run projections of the federal funds rate submitted at the June 2016 meeting was 3 percent. (See www.federalreserve.gov/monetarypolicy/fomcminutes20160615ep.htm.) Out-year projections of the 3-month Treasury bill rate recently published by the Office of Management and Budget (www.whitehouse.gov/sites/default/files/omb/budget/fy2017/assets/17msr.pdf) were also close to 3 percent, as were the ones published by the Congressional Budget Office (www.cbo.gov/about/products/budget economic data#4) early in 2016.

[2] From December 2008 through November 2015, the effective lower bound for the federal funds rate was approximately equal to the mid-point of the FOMC's target range, 0 to 25 basis points. Recently, several foreign central banks have demonstrated that the inconvenience of holding very large amounts of cash makes it feasible to push overnight interest rates somewhat below zero. However, this newly demonstrated ability would not materially increase the extent to which short-term interest rates could be reduced in response to a future recession.

simulate the effects of adverse shocks under different assumptions for monetary policy. This simulation analysis suggests that, even in the event of a fairly severe recession, asset purchases and forward guidance should be able to compensate for the FOMC's likely limited scope to cut short-term interest rates in the future. That said, this analysis also suggests that there could be situations in which this might not be possible.

Monetary Easing During Past Recessions

Historically, the Federal Reserve has responded to recessions by cutting short-term interest rates markedly. As shown in the first column of Table 1, the cumulative reduction in the federal funds rate recorded during the past nine recessions has ranged from almost 3 percentage points during the early-1960s recession to more than 10 percentage points during the 1981-1982 slump, for an average decline of about 5½ percentage points. To a substantial degree, cuts of this magnitude were facilitated prior to the mid-1990s by much higher prevailing rates of inflation than today, which in turn boosted the average level of interest rates. Also important was a higher "equilibrium" real interest rate—R*, the level of the federal funds rate adjusted for inflation that would be consistent with the economy settling down at maximum employment in the absence of shocks. (This rate, plus trend inflation, determines the longer-run normal level of the federal funds rate.) For example, Holston, Laubach and Williams (2016) estimate that R* has recently declined 2 or 3 percentage points from its average level during the 1980s and 1990s.

In addition to these "trend" factors, the scope for policy easing during past downturns was also boosted by cyclical economic considerations in the run-up to the recession. As illustrated by the upper-right panel of Figure 1 and summarized in the second column of Table 1, the real federal funds rate was appreciably above its equilibrium level at the start of the past seven recessions, sometimes markedly so.[3] In most cases, the pre-existing tight stance of policy

appears to have been in response to inflationary pressures, as demonstrated by elevated rates of

core PCE inflation; relatedly, labor market conditions at the start of most of the recessions were

also relatively tight. (See the two rightmost columns of Table 1.) But as labor utilization and

inflation fell, monetary policy reversed course and the real federal funds rate moved from well

above its equilibrium level to (in most cases) well below.

One implication of these historical patterns is that, if the Federal Reserve were to again

encounter conditions similar to those seen in the past (controlling for differences in trend

inflation and R*), then the FOMC's scope for cutting the federal funds rate during a future

recession would presumably be greater than 3 percentage points. In such circumstances, the

FOMC probably would have been tightening prior to the recession, pushing short-term interest

rates above their normal level. For this reason, comparing the amount of easing seen in the past

to the projected average level of the federal funds rate in the future likely understates the

capacity of the FOMC's traditional policy instrument to provide accommodation.

Another problem with using past easing episodes to gauge the FOMC's future scope for

easing is that the structure of the economy has changed over time, potentially altering the amount

of accommodation that would be desirable to provide in the event of a future recession. This

change is most evident in the behavior of inflation. As shown in Figure 1, core PCE inflation

fluctuated markedly prior to the mid-1990s, but since then has been comparatively quite stable,

staying reasonably close to 2 percent; relatedly, core inflation now appears to be much less

sensitive to swings in resource utilization than was previously the case.[4] In addition, evidence

---

[3] Updated R* estimates from the Laubach and Williams (2003) model are used to construct the estimates reported in Table 1 and Figure 1; these estimates are available from www.frbsf.org/economic-research/economists/john-williams. Estimates of R* for the two earlier recessions from this model are not available.
[4] Kiley 2015 and Blanchard (2016) provide overviews of changes in U.S. inflation dynamics since the 1960s.

suggests that the FOMC has become more responsive to movements in real activity and inflation over time, which probably explains in part the increased stability of inflation.[5] Beyond these changes, the interest sensitivity of the economy may have shifted over time as a result of changes in mortgage finance, the growing openness of the economy, and other factors.[6] Finally, and most importantly, the Federal Reserve did not engage in large-scale asset purchases or provide explicit guidance about the future path of the federal funds rate prior to the recent financial crisis.

Assessing the Adequacy of the FOMC's Tools Using Model Simulations

An alternative way to assess the ability of the FOMC to respond to future recessions is to use a model of the U.S. economy to simulate the effects of highly adverse shocks under different assumptions for the response of monetary policy, with the objective of estimating the degree to which asset purchases and forward guidance would be able to compensate for a limited ability to cut the federal funds rate. To this end, we use FRB/US, a macroeconometric model maintained at the Federal Reserve Board for forecasting and policy analysis.[7] For several reasons, FRB/US is well-suited for studying this issue. For one, it provides a good empirical description of the current dynamics of the economy, including the low sensitivity of inflation to movements in real activity. In addition, the model has a detailed treatment of the ways in which monetary policy affects spending and production through changes in financial conditions, including movements in various longer-term interest rates, equity prices, and the foreign exchange value of the dollar. In particular, the model's structure enables it to control for shifts in the (rational) expectations of households and firms about the future paths of short-term interest rates, inflation, and real

---

[5] See Cogley and Sargent (2001).
[6] See Boivin, Kiley and Mishkin (2011).
[7] Full documentation of the FRB/US model is available at www.federalreserve.gov/econresdata/frbus/us-models-about.htm.

activity in response to announced changes in monetary policy. Finally, the model's asset pricing

formulas provide a way for long-term interest rates and other financial factors to respond to

shifts in term premiums induced by the Federal Reserve's large-scale asset purchases.[8]

A severe recession: no forward guidance or asset purchases

The simulation analysis begins by assuming that the economy is initially growing in line

with its long-run trend, accompanied by normal rate of labor utilization, PCE inflation running at

2 percent, and a federal funds rate that is stable at 3 percent. Thus, pre-recession conditions do

not provide any additional scope for reducing the federal funds rate, in contrast to the situation

seen in the run-up to many past downturns. Beginning in year 1, the economy is then buffeted

by a set of adverse shocks that push the economy into recession. This base case is illustrated by

the dotted blue line in the lower-left panel of Figure 2, which shows unemployment climbing to

almost 10 percent after two years, 5 percentage points above baseline. Real activity recovers

only gradually from that point on, and the unemployment rate takes an additional three and half

years to fall back to, and then for a time below, normal. Despite the appreciable period of slack,

inflation falls only modestly to a low of 1½ percent and slowly recovers thereafter.

An economic downturn of this magnitude would be fairly severe and protracted by

historical standards. As shown in Table 2, only two recessions in the past fifty years witnessed a

---

[8] The effects of asset purchases on term premiums used in this study are calibrated to be consistent with the estimates reported in Ihrig et al (2012) and Engen, Laubach and Reifschneider (2015) for the second and third phases of the Federal Reserve's large-scale asset purchase programs, both of which involved buying assets of a longer average maturity (and thus a larger term premium effect) than the original phase. Specifically, the simulations reported here assume that announcing the purchase of an additional $500 billion in longer-term Treasury securities causes an immediate 20 basis point drop in the term premium embedded in the yield on the 10-year Treasury note; for yields on the 5-year Treasury note and the 30-year Treasury bond, the initial decline is assumed to be 17 basis points and 7 basis points, respectively. Thereafter, the downward pressure on term premiums is assumed to decline geometrically at 5 percent per quarter; this rate would be consistent with the Federal Reserve using reinvestments to maintain the size of its portfolio at its new, higher level for several years, and then allowing it to shrink passively by suspending reinvestment.

comparable trough in labor utilization or saw the unemployment rate take so long to return to its natural rate after the recession ended. Moreover, one of those cases (the 1981-1982 recession) was largely a result of the Federal Reserve's forceful efforts to bring inflation under control, and so may have limited relevance for future FOMCs given how stable inflation has been in the past twenty years. Admittedly, the other case—the 2007-2009 recession, which was followed by the slowest recovery since the Great Depression—demonstrates that the illustrative scenario is not necessarily the worst situation that a future FOMC could potentially face, in that it features a considerably faster recovery. Nonetheless, the scenario does provide a fairly tough standard for evaluating the FOMC's ability to respond to future recessions.

In the base-case scenario, the FOMC lowers the federal funds rate to zero during the first year of the recession in response to the sharp rise in unemployment and the modest decline in inflation (blue dotted lines, upper left panel). Short-term interest rates remain stuck at near zero for the next three years, until economic conditions have improved sufficiently to warrant gradually raising the federal funds rate. In setting this path for policy, the FOMC is assumed to follow the prescriptions of a simple rule, $R_t = R^* + \pi_t + 0.5(\pi_t - \pi^*) - 2.0(U_t - U^*)$, subject to the ELB constraint. In this rule, R is the federal funds rate; R* equals 1 percent, the value of the real federal funds rate consistent with stable long-run employment and inflation in the scenario; π is the 4-quarter rate of core PCE inflation; π^* equals 2 percent, the rate of PCE inflation targeted by the FOMC; U is the unemployment rate, and U* equals 4.8 percent, the long-run value of the unemployment rate consistent with stable long-run inflation.[9] Because investors (and the public more generally) understand that monetary policy will follow the constrained prescriptions of the simple policy rule and that the FOMC will not engage in asset

_____

[9] The median of FOMC participants' individual estimates of the longer-run rate of unemployment reported in June 2016 was also 4.8 percent.

purchases, long-term Treasury yields fall moderately at the outset of the recession and gradually

rise thereafter (dotted blue lines, upper right panel).

Hypothetical outcomes without the ELB constraint

Relative to the well-known Taylor (1993) rule, the rule used to set the federal funds rate

in the base-case simulation is twice as aggressive in responding to movements in resource

utilization.[10] Moreover, as discussed in Taylor (1999), a more aggressive rule like this one does

a better job than the Taylor rule in stabilizing output and inflation across a variety of empirical

representations of the economy. But more importantly for the analysis in this study, the rule's

heightened responsiveness to slack is in line with the FOMC's actual behavior in the years prior

to the federal funds rate hitting its effective lower bound in December 2008.[11] For that reason,

the rule can be used as a rough gauge of how much policymakers might hypothetically like to cut

short-term interest rates in response to a future recession of the magnitude considered here, were

they somehow able to push interest rates below zero without limit. As indicated by the dashed

red lines of Figure 2, when the simulation is re-run with the ELB constraint removed, the rule

prescribes lowering the federal funds rate to -6 percent, a full 9 percentage points below

baseline.[12] With the average future level of short-term interest rates now appreciably lower in

---

[10] The Taylor (1993) rule is $R_t = R^* + \pi_t + 0.5(\pi_t - \pi^*) + 0.5y_t$, where the measure of resource utilization y_t is the output gap, defined as the percentage difference between real GDP and its estimated potential level. Because the output gap is approximately equal to $-2(U_t - U^*)$, the Taylor rule is therefore half as responsive to slack as the rule used in the simulations.

[11] For the sample period 2000Q1 to 2008Q4, the value of c_2 in the regression $R_t = c_1 + c_2 U_t + c_3 \pi_t$ is -2.2 when c_3 is constrained to equal 1.5, and -2.4 when c_3 is unconstrained. (In the latter case, c_3 is estimated to be close to zero, in large part because the lack of variation in core PCE inflation during this period means that this parameter cannot be estimated with any precision.) The R^2 of the equation when c_2 is constrained to equal -2.0 and c_3 to equal 1.5 is 0.87, only a bit below its value when all coefficients are left unconstrained.

[12] Such a large reduction in the federal funds rate would be feasible only if the average level of the federal funds rate was 9 percent, implying some combination of a much higher equilibrium real funds rate and a much higher inflation target than that predicted for the future. This is another indication that replicating macroeconomic performance under the unconstrained simple policy rule is a tough standard for judging the efficacy of asset purchases and forward guidance in compensating for a limited ability to cut the federal funds rate in the future.

this simulation than in the constrained case, long-term interest rates decline more noticeably and financial conditions overall become more supportive of growth. As a result, labor market conditions in this hypothetical scenario do not deteriorate as much and recover more quickly, and inflation declines somewhat less.

Overcoming the ELB constraint: results with forward guidance and asset purchases

Could ELB-constrained policymakers replicate or even improve upon these hypothetical outcomes for unemployment and inflation using some combination of forward guidance and asset purchases? To answer this question, a third scenario is run in which policymakers announce at the start of the recession that they will purchase $2 trillion in longer-term Treasury securities. In addition, they depart from the simple policy rule by announcing their intention to pursue a "lower-for-longer" strategy that involves cutting the federal funds rate to its effective lower bound more quickly, keeping it there as long as the unemployment rate is above 5 percent, and then returning to the prescriptions of the policy rule only gradually thereafter. Investors, households and firms are assumed to treat these announced changes to future monetary policy as credible and to fully understand their future economic implications.

As indicated by the solid black lines in Figure 2, these policy changes cause interest rates to fall somewhat more on average than they do in the hypothetical unconstrained case, particularly when adjusted for inflation. Because of the resulting greater improvement in overall financial conditions, monetary policy is not only able to replicate the unconstrained path for the unemployment rate during the first few years of the economic downturn, but is later able to generate relatively stronger labor market conditions; the anticipation of less future slack on average in turn reduces disinflationary pressures during the early years of the downturn.

Overall, these results suggest that, in the event of a future recession, policymakers would indeed be able to use asset purchases and forward guidance to compensate for a limited ability to cut the federal funds rate, even if the economic downturn turned out to be quite severe by historical standards. This finding, however, does not tell us anything about the relative effectiveness of the two nontraditional tools, or the degree to which one could be substituted for the other. Additional simulations (not shown) indicate that the reduction in term premiums accounts for roughly half of the improvement in macroeconomic performance relative to the base case in which constrained policymakers do not engage in either asset purchases or forward guidance. By itself, this result would seem to suggest a substantial tradeoff between asset purchases and forward guidance. But as discussed in Engen, Laubach and Reifschneider (2015), disentangling the effects of the two tools is extremely difficult in practice. The credibility of promises to follow a certain course of action for setting the federal funds rate in the future are almost certainly enhanced by provision of asset purchases today, as the latter are a concrete demonstration of a desire to provide additional accommodation. And the net stimulus provided by asset purchases depends in part on expectations of how policymakers will adjust short-term interest rates in the future in response to the stronger real activity and inflation sparked by lower term premiums in the near term.

Assessing adequacy using a different standard: optimal-control policy

One potential objection to the preceding analysis is that it could understate the degree to which policymakers, if unconstrained, would wish to lower interest rates in response to such a severe recession; if so, then forward guidance and asset purchases would have to do more to make up for the limited ability to cut the federal funds rate. One way to examine this issue is to consider what an "optimal" policy response to the recession might look like in the absence of the

ELB constraint, under which policymakers would be free to adjust the federal funds rate as they wish over time to best achieve some objective.

In the spirit of the dual mandate, let us assume that policymakers would like to minimize the sum of expected future deviations of the unemployment rate from its natural rate and deviations of inflation from the FOMC's 2 percent inflation goal. In addition, let us also assume that policymakers wish to avoid abrupt quarter-to-quarter movements in the federal funds rate in order to reduce the risk of financial market disruptions. Using so-called optimal-control techniques and a model of the economy such as FRB/US, it is possible to compute a path for the federal funds rate that achieves this objective given the adverse shocks hitting the economy.[13] In particular, one can determine the "optimal" amount of conventional easing that policymakers would hypothetically like to undertake by computing the optimal-control path without imposing the ELB constraint. One can then re-compute the optimal path subject to the constraint to see whether it is possible to replicate the unconstrained results for real activity and inflation using the detailed forward guidance implicit in the revised optimal path. Finally, one can introduce an asset purchase program, and see how well the addition of purchases plus a (yet again) revised optimal path does in limiting disinflationary pressures and the rise in unemployment. Crucially for this analysis, the public at the onset of the recession is assumed to have full understanding of both how policymakers will act over time in response to the shocks and the economic implications of those actions in all three cases.

---

[13] Formally, at the start of the recession policymakers seek to find a path for the federal funds rate (R) over the next eighty quarters that minimizes the loss function $L = \sum_{j=1}^{80} \beta^j \left\{ \left(U_j - 4.8 \right)^2 + \left(\pi_j - 2 \right)^2 + \left(\Delta R_j \right)^2 \right\}$, subject to the dynamics of the FRB/US model and the current and future shocks hitting the economy. In this expression, the discount factor β equals .99 and U and π denote the unemployment rate and four-quarter core PCE inflation, respectively. For more information on optimal-control policy in the context of the FRB/US model, see Brayton, Laubach and Reifschneider (2014).

Results from this exercise are reported in Figure 3. Were it possible to drive short-term interest rates below zero without limit, optimal-control policy would call for an appreciably easier stance of monetary policy relative to the prescriptions of the simple policy rule (dashed red lines, Figure 3 compared to Figure 2). In particular, the federal funds rate under this (hypothetical) strategy would decline almost 12 percentage points, to -9 percent, and short-term interest rates would remain below zero for about five years before rising steeply in the out-years. Investors, recognizing how low short-term interest rates will be on average over the coming decade, would push the 10-year Treasury yield down to less than ½ percent at the start of the recession. Reflecting these accommodative financial conditions, the unemployment rate would peak at just under 8 percent and would be back to its normal level within 3½ years. Moreover, inflation would stay quite close to 2 percent.

Not surprisingly, outcomes for real activity and inflation are substantially worse in the more realistic case where short-term rates cannot fall below zero (dotted blue lines). When optimal-control policy is constrained by the ELB, policymakers attempt to compensate by pledging to keep the federal funds rate near zero for longer (over six years) and to raise it by much less on average thereafter relative to the unconstrained case. However, the effectiveness of this strategy for offsetting the effects of the ELB is fairly limited. Relative to the unconstrained optimal case, long-term interest rates decline by much less, thereby providing less support to aggregate demand and so causing unemployment to be higher during the first few years of the downturn. That said, the promise to keep short-term interest rate near zero for many years, and to raise them only gradually thereafter, does succeed in pushing the unemployment rate well below its natural rate for several years later in the decade, and the expectation that the labor market will be relatively tight later for a time in the future helps to keep inflation near 2 percent during the first years of the economic downturn and beyond.

In principle, a policy that promised to keep the federal funds rate near zero for even longer than the constrained optimal policy, and to raise it even more slowly thereafter, would do more to reduce peak unemployment during the recession. But such a strategy would be non-optimal, for two reasons. First, it would tend to push inflation above the 2 percent target. Second, it would cause the unemployment rate later in the decade to fall even lower, which would be undesirable under the assumption that policymakers dislike the unemployment rate falling below its natural rate as much as they dislike it rising above. Whether this assumption accurately reflects policymakers' true preferences is, of course, open to question. But this aspect of optimal-control policy does help to explain why even $4 trillion in asset purchases do so little to improve macroeconomic performance when the federal funds rate path is simultaneously reoptimized (solid black lines). In order to avoid greater undershooting of the unemployment rate later in the decade, and hence higher inflation earlier on, the reoptimized path calls for the federal funds rate to lift off from zero earlier and subsequently to rise more quickly relative to the constrained optimal path without asset purchases. The resultant increase in the expected average value of future short-term interest rates thus works to offset the initial downward pressure on long-term interest rates caused by lower term premiums, thus weakening the net stimulus to the real economy at the start of the recession.

What conclusions should one take away from these optimal-control exercises? On the one hand, they would seem to suggest that asset purchases and highly-explicit forward guidance would be of limited effectiveness in compensating for a reduced scope to cut the nominal federal funds rate in the event of a future recession. On the other hand, the results from these optimal-control experiments rest on some rather extreme assumptions. First, the simulated reductions in the nominal federal funds rate path under unconstrained optimal policy would be feasible only in a world where the average level of the federal funds rate was at least 13 percent, implying that the FOMC's inflation goal would have to be 11 percent or higher. Given that society would almost certainly not tolerate inflation running persistently anywhere near this level because of the costs it would impose, the unconstrained optimal policy is thus a dubious benchmark for gauging the extent to which unconstrained monetary policymakers would like to ease in response to a severe recession. Second, the optimal-control simulations assume that the FOMC at the start of the recession can bind future Committees to follow through on the original plan for the future path of the federal funds rate, even though their future counterparts might prefer to depart from that course by reoptimizing—a situation which would tend to undercut the credibility of the original plan. Finally, the optimal-control simulations assume that policymakers are able to fine-tune expectations about the future course of the federal funds rate under optimal-control policy to a remarkable degree despite the difficulties of communicating an optimal-control strategy in a world in which the outlook is always changing (and with it, the optimal policy). These issues with optimal-control policy suggest that the earlier results generated with the simple policy rule are probably a more informative and realistic way to judge the FOMC's practical ability to respond to a future recession.

Side-bar: the general effectiveness of monetary policy

Before considering some caveats to this assessment, it is worth pausing to reflect on the implications of the preceding analysis for the general effectiveness of monetary policy, constrained or not. Based on the results presented in Figure 2, monetary policy would seem to have only a modest ability to reduce the severity of a recession and to speed up the subsequent recovery, even when it is possible to reduce short-term interest rates dramatically. This conclusion may seem surprising given that, in many past economic downturns, real activity recovered rapidly once the FOMC started easing. But as was noted earlier, tight monetary policy in the run-up to previous economic downturns played an important role in *causing* some past recessions. Thus, it is not surprising that economic growth would pick up once a key factor restraining real activity was reversed by FOMC easing. In this respect, the illustrative recession is similar to the most recent downturn, which was driven by developments that were for the most part independent of the FOMC's actions.[14] Of course, it could be that the FRB/US model understates the efficacy of monetary policy, perhaps because of a failure to fully account for the ability of accommodative policy to influence consumer and business confidence and investors' perceptions of risk in a favorable manner. And in fact, some other models do yield stronger interest-rate effects (Chung, 2015). But the experience of the past seven years would seem to suggest that the interest sensitivity of aggregate spending—broadly defined to include wealth and exchange rate effects—is just not great enough for even very low long-term interest rates to quickly return the economy to full employment.

Secular Stagnation and Other Caveats

Of course, the simulation results reported in Figure 2 may paint an overly optimistic picture about the ability of the Federal Reserve to use forward guidance and asset purchases to compensate for a limited ability to cut the federal funds rate in response to a future recession. In

---

[14] In hindsight, the 2007-2009 recession appears to have been largely attributable to the collapse of a housing bubble whose macroeconomic effects were greatly exacerbated by many overleveraged households and firms and a financial system that was quite vulnerable to shocks. That said, the housing bubble itself may not have been completely independent of monetary policy, in that low short-term interest rates from 2001 through 2005 may have contributed to the rise in house prices during this period. But as discussed by Dokko *et al* (2011), the primary driver of the housing bubble—which was not just a U.S. phenomenon—appears to have been overly lax lending standards. Moreover, the FOMC's decision to keep the federal funds rate low on average during those years was itself motivated by weak underlying economic activity and core PCE inflation that remained subdued.

this regard, one key risk is that future policymakers may have even less room to cut the federal funds rates than currently predicted by forecasters. As Summers (2015) has argued, aging populations, slower productivity growth, and a heightened global reluctance to spend and invest may have pushed the United States and other advanced economies into a state of secular stagnation, in which interest rates will remain extremely low for the foreseeable future unless offset by expansionary fiscal policy. This hypothesis is broadly consistent with updated estimates from the Laubach-Williams model indicating that persistently slow productivity growth in recent years has caused the current value of the real equilibrium federal funds rate, as well as its projected long-run value, to fall to about zero; accordingly, the average value of the nominal federal funds rate in the future might be only 2 percent.[15]

To explore the ramifications of this possibility, one can re-run the simulations using the same adverse shocks but an alternative baseline in which both short- and long-term interest rates prior to the recession are a full percentage point lower than in the base case. As indicated by the dotted blue lines in Figure 4, policymakers who strictly follow the prescriptions of the simple policy rule and eschew asset purchases are now even more constrained than in the base-case simulation considered earlier, resulting in a smaller decline in long-term interest rates, somewhat higher unemployment, and somewhat lower inflation. Despite the reduced scope to cut the federal funds rate, however, monetary policy is still able to provide enough additional accommodation through asset purchases and forward guidance to overcome the effects of the ELB constraint. In this case (solid black lines), outcomes for real activity and inflation are on

[15] The longer-run value of the federal funds rate might also be lower if inflation were to fail to return to 2 percent, contrary to the expectations of forecasters. But given that the current stance of U.S. monetary policy appears to be moderately accommodative and supportive of further increases in labor utilization, this risk seems low as long as policymakers remain committed to achieving the FOMC's inflation objective.

average better than what would hypothetically be obtained if policymakers were free to cut the federal funds rate as much as prescribed by the unconstrained rule (dashed red lines).

The catch to this result is that the volume of asset purchases needed to make up for the ELB constraint has now expanded to $4 trillion—even more than the $3.5 trillion purchased by the FOMC between late 2008 and mid-2014. Of course, policymakers in this situation might instead opt to economize on additional asset purchases by also adopting an even more aggressive lower-for-longer funds rate policy. For example, other model simulations (not shown) suggest that policymakers could achieve approximately the same outcomes for unemployment and inflation by combining $3 trillion in asset purchases with guidance that short-term interest rates will remain near zero until the unemployment rate falls to 4 percent, rather than 5 percent as previously assumed. But that alternative approach would also involve breaking new ground in the use of non-traditional policy tools. In either case, there would be a risk that these tools might not prove to be as effective when pushed this far as the model simulations suggest. For example, the success of the strategy in the simulation rests on being able to reduce term premiums by enough to push long-term Treasury yields down to ½ percent, an unprecedentedly low level that might be difficult to achieve in practice. Moreover, because these rather aggressive strategies would be used to combat an economic downturn that would be considerably less prolonged (although as deep) as that from which we are only now emerging, doubt might arise about the commitment of the FOMC to follow through on its announced plans. If so, the asset purchases and the forward guidance would have less favorable expectational effects, thus reducing their effective stimulus.

Before closing, some other caveats to the earlier analysis should be noted. First, Kiley (2014) presents evidence that the economic stimulus associated with historical movements in term premiums has been less than that associated with movements in the expected path of short-term interest rates. Because term premiums have been influenced over time by a range of factors (each of which may correlate differently with real activity), it may be that his empirical results do not apply to shifts in term premiums induced by large-scale asset purchases. But if they do, then the FRB/US simulations significantly overstate the accommodation that could be provided by this tool.

Second, the simulation analysis assumes that policymakers at the start of the recession immediately announce an asset-purchase program and their intention to pursue a lower-for-longer funds rate strategy, causing an immediate revision to the public's expectations for the future. In reality, however, the policy response to a recession may take time to unfold, in part because policymakers and the public could initially underestimate the ultimate magnitude and persistence of a severe economic downturn, as was case following the financial crisis. As noted by Engen, Laubach and Reifschneider (2015), such recognition lags can diminish considerably the actual stimulus provided by forward guidance and asset purchases. The same holds true if households and firms have only a limited understanding of the economic implications of announced changes in monetary policy.

Finally, the analysis in this paper has focused on the ability of the Federal Reserve to respond to a severe recession at a point in the future when the economy is at full employment, with inflation equal to 2 percent and interest rates running at their normal longer-run levels. Today, however, the economy is not yet fully recovered from the previous recession, with the federal funds rate still very low and the Fed's balance sheet still very elevated. Under these circumstances, the ability of monetary policy to respond to a recession, should one occur in the near term, would be more limited than suggested by the analysis in this paper. And even after the economy has fully recovered, one would not want to rule out the possibility that a future FOMC might have to confront an economic downturn even deeper or more prolonged than the one considered here. Although the risk of such an extreme event seems relatively low, if it did occur, monetary policy on its own would probably be unable to respond as much as would be desirable, implying that accommodative fiscal policy action would be needed.

Conclusion

The federal funds rate now appears likely to settle down over the next few years at a rather low level by historical standards, thereby limiting the ability of future policymakers to support real activity and inflation through lower short-term interest rates in the event of an economic downturn. Nevertheless, even in fairly adverse circumstances the FOMC should be able to compensate by using large-scale asset purchases and "lower-for-longer" forward guidance about the federal funds rate to put additional downward pressure on longer-term interest rates. In particular, model simulations of a severe recession suggest that policymakers would be able to use a combination of federal funds rate cuts, forward guidance, and asset purchases to replicate (and even improve upon) the economic performance that hypothetically would occur were it possible to ignore the zero lower bound on interest rates and cut short-term interest rates as much as would be prescribed by a fairly aggressive policy rule. That said, one cannot rule out the possibility that there could be circumstances in the future in which the ability of the FOMC to provide the desired degree of accommodation using these tools would be strained.

References

Blanchard, Olivier (2016). "The Phillips Curve: Back to the '60s?" *American Economic Review*, Vol. 106(5), pp. 31-34.

Boivin, Jean, Michael T. Kiley, and Frederic S. Mishkin (2011). "How Has the Monetary Transmission Mechanism Evolved Over Time?" *Handbook of Monetary Economics*, Vol. 3a, pp. 369-422.

Brayton, Flint, Thomas Laubach, and David Reifschneider (2014). "Optimal-Control Monetary Policy in the FRB/US Model". FED Notes 2014-11-21. Board of Governors of the Federal Reserve System (U.S.).

Chung, Hess (2015). "The Effects of Forward Guidance in Three Macro Models," FEDS Notes 2014-02-26. Board of Governors of the Federal Reserve System (U.S.).

Cogley, Timothy and Thomas J. Sargent (2001). "Evolving Post-World War II U.S. Inflation Dynamics," *NBER Macroeconomics Annual*, Vol. 16(1), (Cambridge, Mass.: MIT Press), pp. 331-373.

Dokko, Jane, Brian M. Doyle, Michael T. Kiley, Jinill Kim, Shane Sherlund, Jae Sim, and Skander J. Van den Heuvel (2011). "Monetary Policy and the Global Housing Bubble," *Economic Policy*, vol. 26, no. 66, pp. 233-283.

Engen, Eric M., Thomas Laubach, and David Reifschneider (2015). "The Macroeconomic Effects of the Federal Reserve's Unconventional Monetary Policies," Finance and Economics Discussion Series 2015-005. Board of Governors of the Federal Reserve System (U.S.).

Holston, Kathryn, Thomas Laubach, and John C. Williams (2016). "Measuring the Natural Rate of Interest: International Trends and Determinants," Working Paper Series 2016-11. Federal Reserve Bank of San Francisco.

Ihrig, Jane, Elizabeth Klee, Canlin Li, Brett Schulte, and Min Wei (2012). "Expectations about the Federal Reserve's Balance Sheet and the Term Structure of Interest Rates." Finance and Economics Discussion Series 2012-57. Board of Governors of the Federal Reserve System (U.S.).

Kiley, Michael T. (2014). "The Aggregate Demand Effects of Short- and Long-Term Interest Rates," *International Journal of Central Banking*, vol. 10, no. 4, pp. 69-104.

_____ (2015). "Low Inflation in the United States: A Summary of Recent Research," FED Notes 2015-11-23. Board of Governors of the Federal Reserve System (U.S.).

Laubach, Thomas, and John C. Williams (2003). "Measuring the Natural Rate of Interest," *Review of Economics and Statistics*, vol. 85, no. 4, pp. 1063-1070.

Summers, Lawrence H. (2014). "U.S. Economic Prospects: Secular Stagnation, Hysteresis, and the Zero Lower Bound." *Business Economics*, vol. 49 (April), pp. 65-73.

John B. Taylor (1993). "Discretion versus Policy Rules in Practice." *Carnegie-Rochester Conference Series on Public Policy*, vol. 39 (December), pp. 195-214.

_____ (1999). "Introduction" in John B. Taylor, ed., *Monetary Policy Rules* (Chicago: University of Chicago Press), pp. 1-14.

Table 1. Extent of Conventional Monetary Easing During Past Recessions and Accompanying Economic Conditions

NBER Recession Dates	Cumulative Reduction in the Federal Funds Rate (basis points)[1]	Level of the Federal Funds at the Start of Easing Relative to Normal Level (basis points)[2]	Peak Rate of 12-Month Core PCE Inflation During the Recession (percent)	Labor Utilization at the Start of the Recession (percent)[3]
August 1957 to April 1958	287	—	3.2[4]	1.3
April 1960 to February 1961	283	—	2.1	0.3
December 1969 to November 1970	548	46	4.8	2.4
November 1973 to March 1975	770	304	10.2	1.4
January 1980 to July 1980	479	316	9.1	0.2
July 1981 to November 1982	1038	711	8.8	-1.0
July 1990 to March 1991	525	165	4.3	0.4
March 2001 to November 2001	475	193	2.0	0.8
December 2007 to June 2009	513	194	2.3	-0.1

1. For recessions prior to 1990, the cumulative reduction is the difference between the maximum and minimum monthly average of the effective federal funds rate during the period extending from six months prior to the start of the recession to six months after it ends. For the other recessions, the periods of continuous reductions in the intended federal funds rate are June 1990 to January 2002, December 2000 to January 2002, and August 2007 to December 2008.
2. Difference between the federal funds rate (less the 12-month percent change in the core PCE price index) and its real equilibrium value (R*) using the methodology described in Laubach and Williams (2007). Figures in the table are calculated using updated R* estimates from the Laubach-Williams model, available at www.frbsf.org/economic-research/economists/john-williams/.
3. CBO estimate of the long-run natural rate of unemployment minus the actual unemployment rate.
4. Four-quarter percent change in the chain-weighted PCE price index.

Table 2. Labor Utilization During Past Recessions[1]

NBER Recession Dates	Cyclical Trough (percent)	Number of Months for Utilization to Reach Cyclical Trough After Start of Recession	Number of Months for Utilization to Return to Normal After Cyclical Trough[2]
August 1957 to April 1958	-2.1	15	8
April 1960 to February 1961	-1.6	13	9
December 1969 to November 1970	-0.2	12	0
November 1973 to March 1975	-2.8	18	31
January 1980 to July1980	-1.6	6	—[3]
July 1981 to November 1982	-4.7	16	55
July 1990 to March 1991	-2.1	23	29
March 2001 to November 2001	-1.3	27	21
December 2007 to June 2009	-5.0	22	70

1. Labor utilization equals CBO estimate of the long-run natural rate of unemployment minus the actual unemployment rate.
2. Labor utilization is assumed to have returned to normal once it rises above -0.2 percent.
3. Labor utilization did not rise above -0.2 percent prior to the start of the next recession.

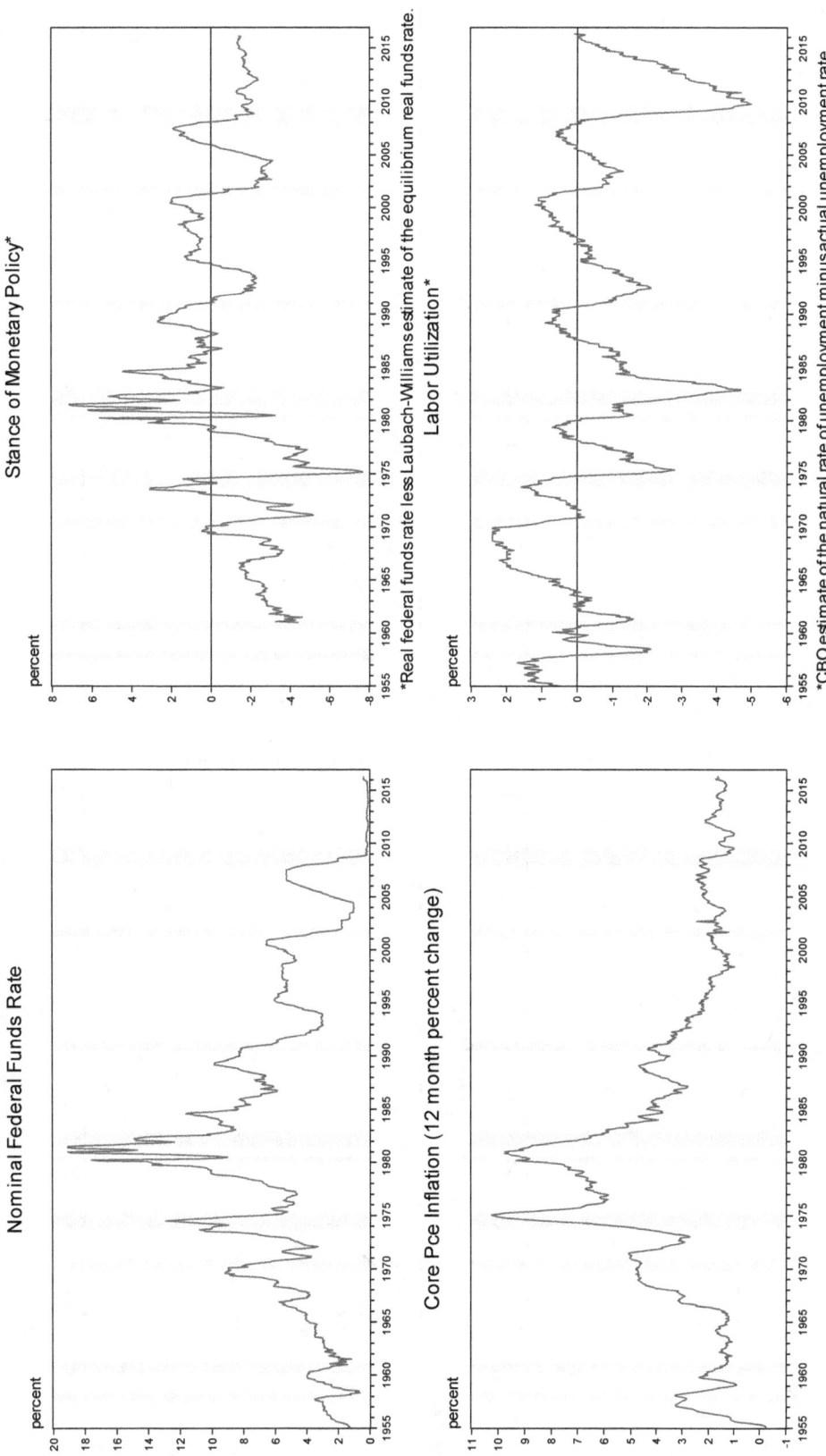

Figure 1. Monetary Easing During Past Recessions and Accompanying Economic Conditions

Nominal Federal Funds Rate

Stance of Monetary Policy*

Core Pce Inflation (12 month percent change)

Labor Utilization*

*Real federal funds rate less Laubach-Williams estimate of the equilibrium real funds rate.

*CBO estimate of the natural rate of unemployment minus actual unemployment rate.

Figure 2. Using Lower-for-Longer Forward Guidance and $2 Trillion in Asset Purchases
to Compensate for a Limited Ability to Reduce the Federal Funds Rate During a Recession

- - - - constrained policy rule — - — unconstrained policy rule ——— constrained policy rule with forward guidance and asset purchases

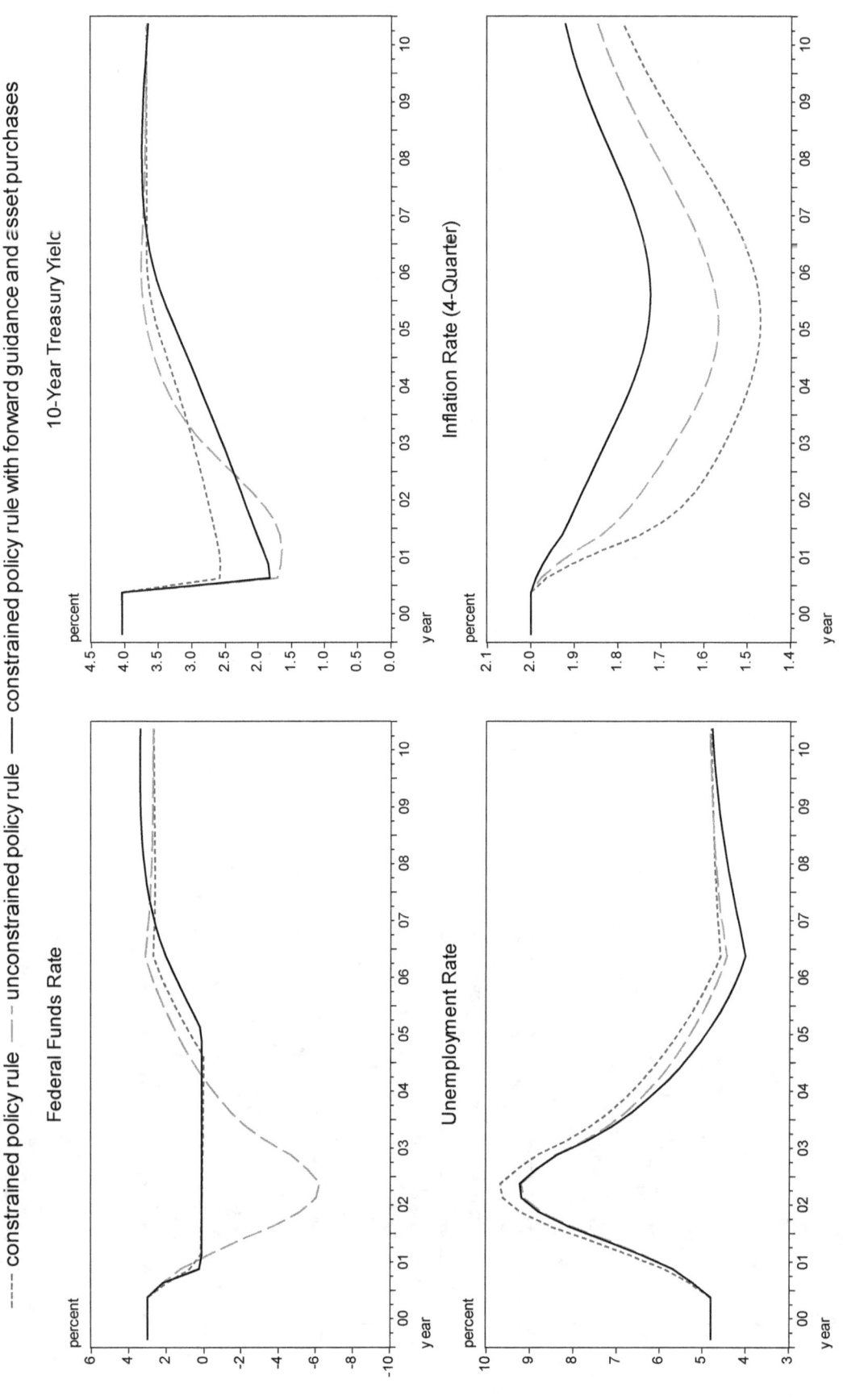

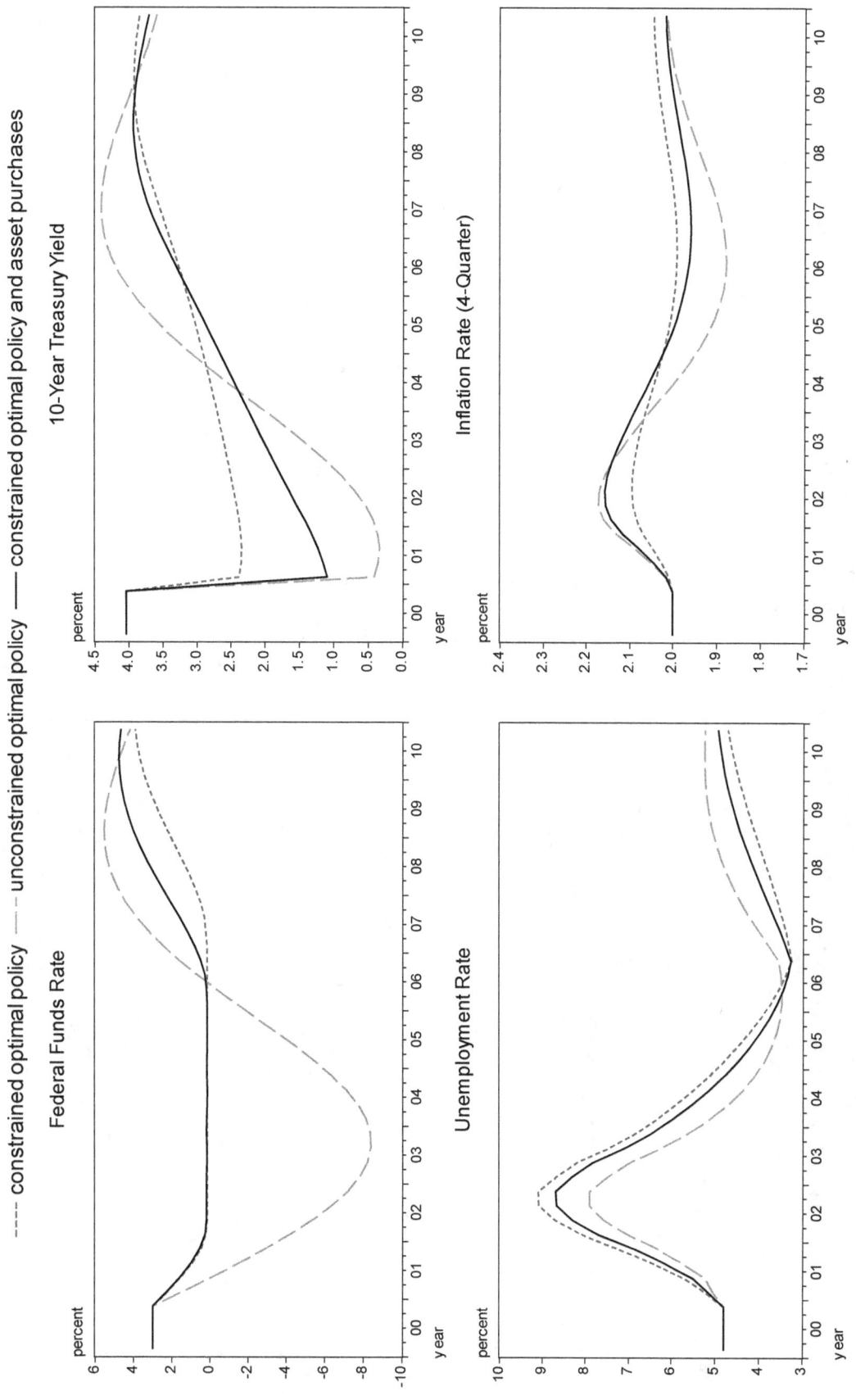

Figure 3. Using $4 Trillion in Asset Purchases to Compensate for a Limited Ability to Optimally Reduce the Federal Funds Rate During a Recession

---- constrained optimal policy ---- unconstrained optimal policy —— constrained optimal policy and asset purchases

Figure 4. Using Lower-for-Longer Forward Guidance and $4 Trillion in Asset Purchases
to Compensate for an Extremely Limited Ability to Reduce the Federal Funds Rate During a Recession

---- constrained policy rule ——— unconstrained policy rule — — constrained policy rule with forward guidance and asset purchases

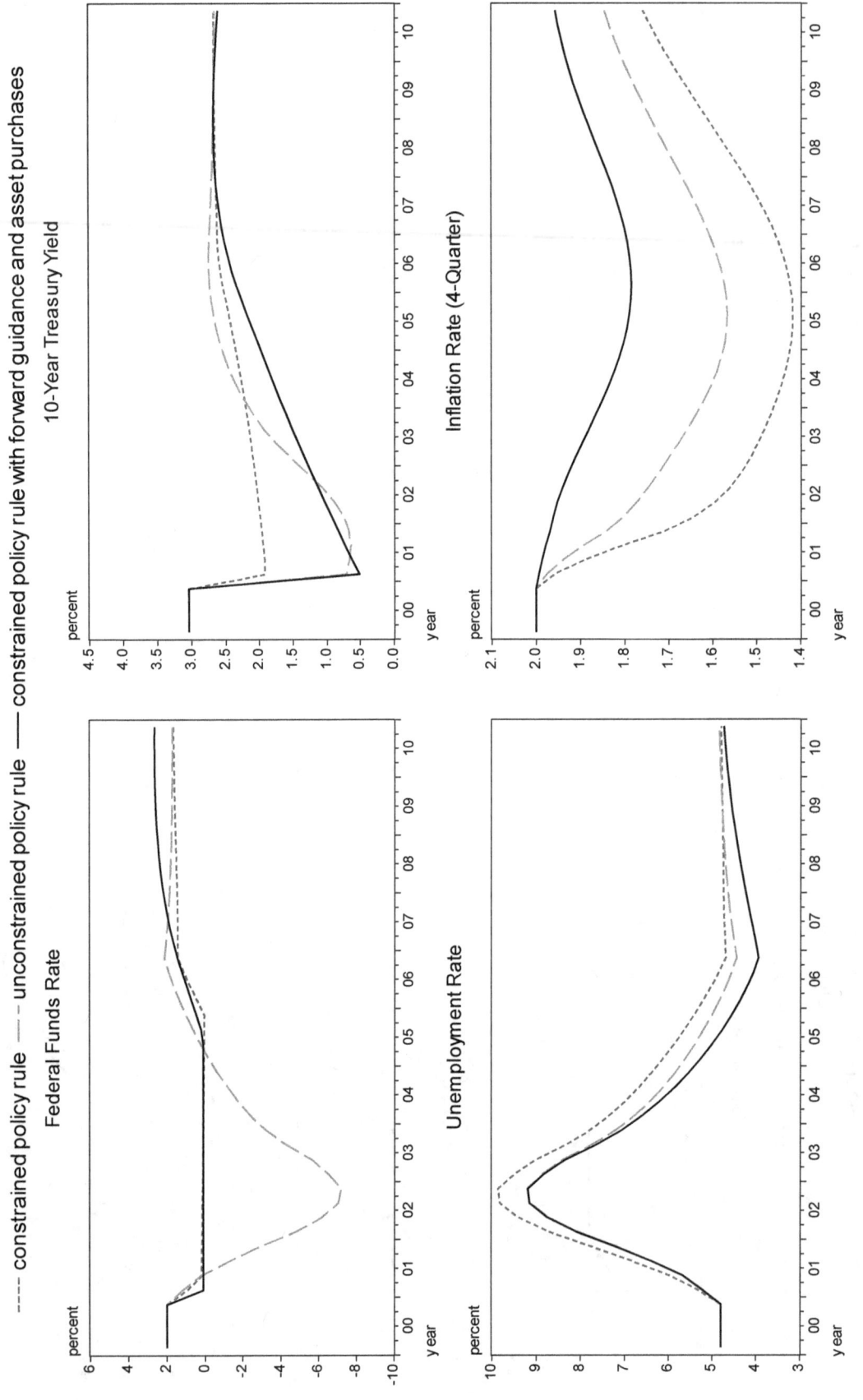